The Roots of an Entrepreneur

John Leslie Gibson

Kingdom Builders Publications LLC

If you don't believe money grows on trees, you are either planting the wrong seeds, or you are planting them in the wrong soil.

JOHN LESLIE GIBSON

© 2019 John Leslie Gibson
The Roots of an Entrepreneur
Kingdom Builders Publications, LLC

All rights reserved. No part of this book may be reproduced or transmitted in any form or by any means without written permission from the author.

Printed in the USA

ISBN
978-0-578-44556-4

Library of Congress Control Number
2019936679

Authored by
John Leslie Gibson

Editor
Kingdom Builders Publications
Lakisha S. Forrester

Cover Design
LoMar Designs

This Book Belongs to

DEDICATION

This book is dedicated to my mother, Susan Elizabeth Bailey Gibson Preston, who gave me the gift of life and taught me how to preserve and appreciate it. To my son, John L. Gibson Jr., who taught me how to be a better man. To my darling wife, Doncella (Donnie) Peeples Gibson, who showed me that the manifestation and transformation of dreams into reality are inspired through study and hard work. To my daughters, Shawnee' Nicole Peeples and Monique Suzanne Gibson Sandiford, who have shown me the type of love that only a daughter can show to a father.

This Book Belongs to

DEDICATION

This book is dedicated to my mother, Susan Elizabeth Bailey Gibson Preston, who gave me the gift of life and taught me how to preserve and appreciate it. To my son, John L. Gibson Jr., who taught me how to be a better man. To my darling wife, Doncella (Donnie) Peeples Gibson, who showed me that the manifestation and transformation of dreams into reality are inspired through study and hard work. To my daughters, Shawnee' Nicole Peeples and Monique Suzanne Gibson Sandiford, who have shown me the type of love that only a daughter can show to a father.

CONTENTS

DEDICATION	III
CONTENTS	5
ACKNOWLEDGMENTS	7
FOREWORD	8
INTRODUCTION	9
I KNOW YOU! YOU'RE AN ENTREPRENEUR!	11
WINNERS, LOSERS, AND SURVIVORS	14
GRANNY	20
THE DAYS I YEARN	25
AS FAR AS I COULD SEE	27
THE MAN ON THE CLOUD	29
MY SAFETY NET HAS A HOLE IN IT	35
FOLLOW THE SIGNS	39
MOVING ON	45
JUMP STREET	49
THE MAN DOWNSTAIRS	53
I'M A HUSTLER	59
THE HOUSEMAN ALWAYS WINS	61
MIDNIGHT THUNDER	68
MOMMA DON'T TAKE NO MESS	74
POISON IN THE WELL	79
ABOUT THE AUTHOR	82

JOHN LESLIE GIBSON

ACKNOWLEDGMENTS

I would like to acknowledge my brother, Bruce Gibson, who saved me from myself at a dangerous time in my life. Thank you for helping me to see that I am a special and unique individual in this world with a specific purpose in life and for recognizing my talent for writing. You are and always will be my best friend. Thanks to my brother, Walter Gibson, who was my protector when we were growing up and my advisor in adulthood.

I would like to acknowledge my brothers, Timothy A. Gibson and Farod Preston, for inspiring me to live an exemplary life. Thanks to my sister, Alice A. Gibson Larry, for being a mother figure when Mom had to go out and work. A special thanks to my friend, Philip Pinckney, who encouraged me and showed me, by example, what the fruit of one's labor really looks like. Thanks to all of my many relatives and friends who have merged pieces of their character with mine to make me who I am.

Last but certainly not least, a special thanks to Melanie Dees and Jerlene Noble for consulting with me and making this book possible; and a special thanks to Louise Smith, the President/Owner of Kingdom Builders Publications for not giving up on the publication of my first book.

FOREWORD

I used to think that people who wrote autobiographies were narcissistic, self-centered, and boring people who didn't have anything to talk about other than themselves. I failed to realize the possibility that their lives may be so filled with interesting experiences and people with rich characters, until they are excited about sharing their lives with others.

After all, to tell a tale of one's own experiences is to tell a tale of others. The birth of a newborn child, for instance, is the core of many conversations by parents, grandparents, and siblings. How can anybody tell a tale of just one's self and not integrate others into their story? That would surely be a boring tale.

So, as I write my story and reflect back on those who I consider to be heroes, villains, and no named people, I will attempt to stop time long enough to concentrate on the theme and flow of my storyline. But, if I get off track and find myself going off on a tangent, please bear with me because sometimes life moves at various paces and it gets difficult to keep up with one's self.

INTRODUCTION

My name is John L. Gibson Sr. I am named after my grandfather, my biological father's father. I call him my biological father because if the truth is to be told, my father was not there for me during my developmental stages in life. I have always resented him for that because I have had friends with fathers who protected them and provided for them in ways that no one did for me.

Like many young men, I have had to grow up without a blueprint for the fundamental development of life, which has caused me to toil through life with trial and error. However, I was more fortunate than many. At least I knew something about my father and his father before him. Knowing something about your own family history is important.

The more you know, the better off you are. Genealogy gives you insight into the depths of your own existence. A runaway father cuts off the roots of a child's history, much like the slave masters did to the black man during slavery, some four hundred years ago. I guess you can say that a runaway father perpetuates the conditions associated with slavery, which still exist right here in America today. Conditions, such as crime, teenage pregnancy, as well as the overpopulation of prison inmates, which consist disproportionately of African American men between the ages of eighteen and twenty-five.

Am I still angry? No, because life has been a learning experience for me which I would like to share with the young men that are coming up today without a father. A father is supposed to be a light on his children's path in life. Because I did not have that light, I had to find my own light. A preacher once told me, "The spotlight of heaven shines on everybody."

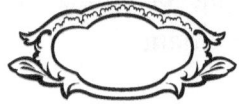

I KNOW YOU! YOU'RE AN ENTREPRENEUR!

In order to be successful at anything in this life, you must love what you do enough to do it for free. Once you find the one thing in your life that you love enough to do for free, you will find yourself doing it every day. Anything that you love enough to do every day will eventually become something that you will become a master of. People will see you, recognize you, and identify you; maybe not so much by your name, appearance, or what you say, but by what you do. You are what you do. That is who you are. They will stop you on the street and say, "I know you. You are that guy or that woman who does such and such."

The first job I ever had was shining shoes. I learned how to shine shoes by observing my two older brothers. We would go from bars to street corners. We would get down on our knees and shine shoes for a quarter. Some people would refer to us as the poor boys. But, there was more to us than meets the human eye. My brothers and I had a purpose. Our purpose was to protect our family from starvation. That was our way of raising a few dollars to help our single mother defray her household expenses accumulated from the demands of her five children's basic needs.

Speaking of basic needs, most people don't really know the difference between a need and a want. In order to pursue anything in this life, you have to have a motive. You have to have a reason to do whatever you do. All movement requires motive. Your heart beats to move blood throughout your body. If you do not have a good reason for doing the things that you do, then you probably should not do them. Some things might even require more than one reason.

Talk about pulling yourself up by the bootstraps. We did it. It was all basic training for me. I learned how to achieve at an early age. Being deprived of life's basic needs is a harsh motivator, but it is also a dynamic form of inspiration.

I learned early in life that four quarters equal a dollar. Shining shoes and basic arithmetic helped me to understand that if I shined four people's shoes, I would have a dollar. The tips were of great interest to me. The more shoes I shined, the more dollars I would earn. Show me how to make a dollar, and I will do it a million times.

Every now and then, I would run out of supplies. Without the shoe polish that I needed to shine shoes, I couldn't make my money. So, I had to figure out a way to get more money to buy the supplies I needed, in order to keep my inventory in stock.

I observed the older down and outers in the neighborhood who would collect beer and soda cans and cash them in to buy their beverages. I copied their efforts, but instead of buying beverages, I bought supplies to shine shoes. My efforts taught me the meaning of supply and demand.

When you are out there in the world trying to make your way, somebody will notice you and do whatever is necessary to assist you. Sometimes, you won't even know where the help came from. Some people will just want to give you a little boost along the way. Fools call that sort of unseen assistance, luck. Wise men recognize a blessing, even when they don't see where it came from. Just because you do not see something, does not mean it doesn't exist.

    Not all planted seeds grow. Some of them die in the ground. But, all dead things become fertilizer. The more seeds you plant, the greater the odds are that something will grow.

Chapter 1
WINNERS, LOSERS, AND SURVIVORS

You can always tell when you are on your way to hell by the people you meet along the way. The same holds true of paradise.

Wherever your travels may take you throughout your entire life, you will only encounter three types of people, regardless of their age, race, sexual orientation or National Origin. Those three types are: winners, losers, and survivors.

There are distinguishing characteristics that set these three types apart from one another. For instance, if you were to throw all three types of people into a deep, dark hole, taking into consideration how difficult it would be to throw a winner into a deep, dark hole, but if it were to happen, the winner would be the first to get out every time.

Now the survivor, on the other hand, would discover electricity to build a refrigerator to keep his beverages cold, concoct a television and a radio to keep in touch with the outside world. The survivor would make the best of his current situation by providing himself with all the amenities life has to offer.

The loser, being true to his nature, will come to the survivor for his every need, asking, "What's on TV? You got anything to eat? I'm thirsty. What's in the refrigerator to drink?" Then, when the winner returns with help to get the survivor and the loser out of the hole, like a winner would do, the loser, being true to his nature will turn on the survivor, proclaiming, "I don't need you!"

Tonight when the sky is black and the stars and the moon are set, look up towards the heavens and realize that we are all in a deep, dark hole. Then, ask yourself the question, "What type am I? Am I a winner, a loser, or a survivor?" If your conscience is not at peace with your answer, then it is time to make the necessary adjustments within yourself to become the man or woman your Creator created you to be.

"What type is that?" you might ask. Well, let me attempt to answer your question the best I can. Have you ever been in a dark place, so dark until you could not see your own hand if you held it up in front of your own face? Do you believe if you stay in that darkness long enough, your eyes will eventually adjust to that darkness and you will be able to see, if nothing else, shadows?

If your belief system will not allow you to believe you can see light, even in total darkness, then close your eyes for a moment. It might look pitch dark to you at first. But, give it time. Even with your eyes closed, you will eventually see shadows, because no matter how dark it gets, any light will pierce the darkness. You have a light inside of you. We all do. That light is the light of Christ. It is in you, whether you want to acknowledge Him or not.

I won't get all preachy on you because I want you to continue to read and hear what I have to say, and I really don't want you to turn away. So, let me show you the light in a more shaded area.

When you are faced with a problem that you have never been faced with before and you don't quite know what to do, you may call out for help from whomsoever might hear you. The message of Psalm 107 can be helpful in this time of need. Like a friend of mine, who I grew up with named Frank Spivey used to say, "If you holler loud enough, somebody got to hear you. If nobody hears you, it is simply because you did not holler loud enough."

Well, when you are faced with such a dilemma, and you get an idea as to how to deal with that problem, what actually happens at that moment is that a light actually flashes in your brain. That flash is caused by the connecting of two neurons in your brain, creating the birth of an idea, better known as enlightenment. We all have that power within us, even the most dim-witted person among us.

Have you ever seen the mystical image of an angel with a bright halo around her head, casting a light around her entire body, creating a bright aura? That is the image of an enlightened being in a dark place. We human beings are the creatures, which such an image attempts to represent. So, as you walk through the valley of the shadow of death, fear no evil. For, thou art with you (Psalm 23).

There is a lot of truth to the old adage, "Necessity is the mother of invention." Some people only do what they have to do. It would require a fire to get some people to move out of their house, even if that house is in the most deplorable condition in the worse section of town.

The way of the wicked is as darkness: they know not at what they stumble. Proverbs 4:19

Chapter 2
GETTING OUT OF THE HOLE

You can see further from outside of a hole than you can see from inside a hole. If you are in a financial hole or any kind of a hole for that matter, your first reaction and your first gut instinct should be to reach up, grab whatever is within your reach, and pull yourself up and out. The first evidence of a true entrepreneur is the ability to solve a problem. Like a seed, bursting out of the ground, no matter what your life's situation is, there is always room for improvement and there should be a desire to find it. Always do the best you can at everything you do, as often as you can, and the only way you can move is up and forward. The first apparent signs of an entrepreneur are in the early stages of a child's life. A parent who fails to demonstrate healthy examples of good work ethics instills in that child a slothful personality. A lazy child grows up to become a lazy adult. Ambition is not taught; it is innate.

"Grannie, why does your food always taste so much better than the food in the school cafeteria?" a young boy asked his grandmother.

"Because I always add a special ingredient in my food that the people in the school cafeteria do not add," replied his grandmother.

"What's that?" asked the young boy.

"I always add love to my food," the grandmother replied.

Chapter 3
GRANNY
(I is for Independence)

People have asked me on more than one occasion if there has ever been a time in my life when I genuinely felt loved. Each time I am asked that question, my mind rewinds back to my childhood days to my grandmother.

It was a few weeks before it was time for me to start kindergarten and my grandmother was trying to teach me how to tie my shoes. After a few attempts, I was ready to give up. "I can't do it. Why can't you do it for me like you always do?" I asked my grandmother. I did not understand what the big deal was about me learning how to tie my own shoes.

"You are going into kindergarten and the other boys and girls will laugh at you if you don't know how to tie your shoes. You don't want the other kids to laugh at you, do you?"

It was then that I realized my grandmother was on my side, whatever it meant to have someone on your side. But, I knew at that moment, right then and there, that my grandmother cared enough about me to think about what could happen to me before it happened. She cared enough to try to prevent me from being laughed at. That was the first time in my whole entire life that I felt cared about without anyone saying that they cared.

When someone cares about you, he or she don't have to say it. You can feel it. At that time in my life, I had two older brothers, Chuck, who is two years older than Bruce, who is two years older than I am. Then, there is my sister, Antoinette, who is the oldest of us all.

 My three younger brothers, Tim, Fuquan, and Farod, had not yet been born. At that time, I was the baby of the family and my grandmother was trying to prepare me for my new world.

I could see clearly, through my eyes as a 4½-year-old, that it was important to my grandmother that I learned how to tie my shoes, and I did not want to disappoint her. So, I became equally determined to learn how to tie my shoes, as she was to teach me. Before my mother and father came home from work that day, my grandmother taught me and I learned how to tie my shoes.

When my mother and father came home, I told them that Granny had taught me how to tie my shoes.

"That's nice," my mother said, as she began to prepare supper. "Don't you want to see?" I asked my mother as I attempted to get her attention with my newfound skill. But, she was too busy. By that time, my father was watching a baseball game on TV, and I knew not to disturb him. So, I just went to my bedroom and waited for Chucky and Bruce to come home from school. I was so eager to show them what I learned. As I waited, I began to think to myself, "What's taking them so long? They are usually home by now unless they stayed late for after-school activities."

Antoinette was the first to come home. I heard her as she said "hello" to my father, then to Granny and Mom. I came running out of my room to greet my sister. "What's wrong with you?" she asked.

I guess she was surprised because I never seemed so glad to see her before. I wanted to show my sister that I knew how to tie my shoes.

Antoinette just said, "That's nice," and went to her room and turned on her music. Nobody seemed to think anything of the fact that I knew how to tie my shoes. Nobody but Granny and me.

I went back to my bedroom, lied across my bed, and cried myself to sleep. Shortly afterwards, I was awakened by a commotion in the living room. Chuck and Bruce were home.

It appeared that Chuck got bit by a dog. He said that he was riding his bike down the street when a big dog came out from nowhere and bit him. I thought something was strange about that story. "Why would he be riding his bike from school, when he did not ride it to school?" I thought to myself.

My mother believed his story and she went to the owner of the dog's house and started arguing with the lady for not having her dog on a leash. The lady tried to explain to my mother that Chuck was in her yard teasing the dog. But, my mother was not hearing anything the lady had to say. The lady became real apologetic. In an attempt to avoid any further confrontation with my mother, she told her she would absorb all of the medical expenses.

Afterwards, I asked Chuck what really happened. He told me the truth. He and Bruce were playing in the lady's yard, teasing the dog and racing to see who could leap over the fence to get out of the yard before the dog could catch them. It turned out that Bruce got away, but the dog caught Chuck and bit him on his backside.

I could not believe he had gotten so much attention for doing something so wrong, yet no one even cared about me learning how to tie my shoes. But, it all taught me a serious lesson beyond learning how to tie my shoes. It taught me that what I learn and the good that I do is not for others but for me. Granny gave me a really special gift the day she taught me how to tie my shoes. She taught me how to be independent and not to depend on others to do for me what I can do for myself. Also, while I was learning how to tie my shoes, my brother was getting into trouble. Even though my mother did not catch him, the dog did. I guess he learned a lesson that day too.

Chapter 4
THE DAYS I YEARN

Here I am
Dressed in a dream
Ripened by the iridescent lights of age
At least, so it seems.

My youth snatched away
In an instant;
Never to return.

Those days of having my head buried in my Grandma's bosom,
And waking up to the smell
Of her hot cakes cooking.
Gone are the days for which I yearn.

When my grandmother died, everything changed. I did not know how much my mother depended on my grandmother to be there to help raise us and to take care of us while she went to work. After my mother and father separated, it all happened so fast until I really didn't even recognize what was going on until years later. It really isn't fair the way adults alter their children's lives without them having any say in the matter. My father just upped and left one night. I remember him packing his yellow and burgundy suitcase and leaving without even saying goodbye.

Our father's abandoning the family led to consequences which affected our mother, my siblings, and me more than it did my father, at least as far as I could see.

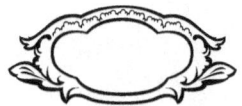

Chapter 5
AS FAR AS I COULD SEE

I had an itch. Not like the one you get from bed bugs or chickenpox. No! That could be soothed with calamine lotion. My itch was the kind of itch that you get in the center of your back that can only be satisfied with manicured fingernails; and for me, Mary was it.

We discovered each other in the back seat of an abandoned 1953 Chevrolet. Well, it wasn't exactly abandoned. My Uncle Russell gave it to my oldest brother, Chuck, for his seventeenth birthday, though he hadn't turned quite seventeen yet.

So, the old car stayed parked in the backyard most of the time, except for on those rare occasions when Chuck and Bruce practiced driving the car up and down the driveway. Never getting license plates or a registration, the old car was just used for banging up against the wall, which divided our yard from our neighbor's yard.

Although the old '53 Chevy never knew a paved road with my brothers behind the wheel, Mary and I went much too far in the back seat of that car. We became best friends, playing the games that poor kids play, having snowball fights, and sleigh riding on the snow covered hills behind Saint Matthews Catholic School. We enjoyed listening to music together and dancing just the two of us. If it wasn't for that itch that kept returning, we could have had a childhood together.

We kept finding ourselves alone together. Then, Mary got pregnant. I felt pushed out, like I was no longer important to her. It was like she had something else to care about, or shall we say someone else to care about.

I didn't even have time to be jealous. The old men at the barbershop started telling me that I was too young to father a child. I was only 15 years old and in the council of fools. They didn't know me, and I was too young to know myself. I was just a foolish kid trying to be grown without guidance, learning life through trial and error.

The impetus of my thoughts was money. I thought that if only I could get enough, then everything would be alright. After all, the people on television looked happy. What I needed was my Grandmother. What I needed was a scolding.

Chapter 6
THE MAN ON THE CLOUD

I don't remember much about the day it all began. But, I do remember coming into the kitchen when my grandmother was humming a familiar gospel hymn. It may have been "Amazing Grace." I'm not sure. She always hummed some spiritual while she was baking, cleaning, or ironing. She was baking a chocolate cake that day. She let me lick the icing off the mixing spoon.

My grandmother was an extremely religious woman and strong spirited. God was her explanation for everything. That particular morning, while I was licking the icing, I noticed a strange-looking insect on the window seal.

"Look Grannie, a bug!" I exclaimed.

I had never seen a bug that looked like that before, and I wanted to kill it. But, my grandmother quickly explained to me that the bug was no ordinary bug. It was in fact a praying mantis.

"What's a praying mantis?" I asked.

My grandmother explained to me that a praying mantis is a special creature created by God to pray for mankind. I must have been bored or just grown weary of my grandmother's explanations about "God this and God that." I don't know exactly what I was feeling at that moment, but my actions, looking back at them from an adult's perspective, reveals that I was feeling a bit testy. Whatever the motive behind the action then is irrelevant now. But, the fact remains until this day, that as soon as my grandmother turned her back towards me, I slammed the window down on that bug, killing it. God have mercy on whomever he had come to pray for on that particular day.

My grandmother turned around with a speed that I had never seen her move at before or ever again after that moment. She reached for me, but I swiftly escaped her grasp. She shouted at me as I ran outside, "You are bad. Evil! You are a bad boy."

I ran until I was outside in the serenity of my backyard. I sat on the underside of a kitchen sink that was turned upside down. I sat and stared up into the sky. I stared and stared as if it was the first time I had ever seen the sky. It may have very well been the first time.

I have told people on several occasions about what

happened next. But, judging from the expressions on their faces, most people think I was imagining things. It is possible, because of my grandmother's religious influence; I may very well have imagined what I believe I saw. But, what I saw was a man standing on a cloud.

He spoke to me and said, "Your grandmother is trying to teach you right from wrong. She wants you to grow up and to do the right thing. Learn to listen to your grandmother. You be a good boy. Do you hear me? I'm going to be watching you!" And then, he was suddenly gone.

I have often looked up to the sky, looking for the man on the cloud, but I have never seen him since that day. That day was a spellbinding day, and I have looked up to the sky for instructions ever since.

My first airplane ride, oddly enough, took my mind back to that childhood experience. I was taking pictures of the clouds when the man sitting on the seat next to me asked me if it was my first time flying. I admitted that is was. We talked for a long time about different things. I was on my way to Nassau in the Bahamas. This was my first vacation that I saved enough money to take. I was going through a dark time in my life, and I was determined to snap myself out of it.

The man on the plane told me that he was a Wall Street Bank president. I told him that I was surprised that a man of his caliber and stature would even bother to talk to an ordinary person like me. He laughed and said, "Whenever I start thinking like that, I usually excuse myself and go to the restroom." I returned the laugh. It felt good talking with that stranger. He was the beginning of the best vacation of my life. That vacation changed my life and I have often wished I had gotten that banker's name and the name of the bank where he worked. Talking with him brought back memories of that day when I met the man on the cloud. Oddly enough, I began looking out the window for him.

Before I took that trip to the Bahamas, I had actually contemplated suicide. I thought I was ready to die. I don't know what sent me into such a deep depth of despair, but there I was. I would sit on my mother's steps leading from her back porch into her yard and stare into space for hours. My brother Bruce would sit beside me, look into the direction in which I was staring, and ask me, "What are you looking at?" He tried hard to make me laugh. Sometimes, it would work, but I was way out on the ledge. Bruce tried to pull me in.

One day I decided to take a ride. I had gone to the Watchung Mountains in Watchung, New Jersey, not far from where I lived in Plainfield, armed with a .38 snub-nose revolver. I was a single parent, with not much of a social life. It was hard for me to develop a relationship, because I had the responsibility of raising my son. I didn't have much time or resources to do much other than work. I was confused and mad at myself for letting myself get into such a rut. I remember a motivational speaker named Joe Bernardino once said, "The only difference between a rut and a grave is the depth." Or, maybe he said, "The death." I'm not sure.

So, I parked my car in a secluded location near a stream of water, and I told myself, "This is it. This is where and how it all ends." And then, as clear as the sight of the man on the cloud, I heard a voice speak to me. The voice said, "Get out of the car." At first, I thought it was the police. But, when I looked around, I didn't see anyone. Then, I recognized the voice. It was the same voice of the man on the cloud. Surely, he had been watching me. "Leave the gun," the voice instructed me.

I left the gun sitting on the front seat in clear view of anyone walking by. But, no one walked by, not to my knowledge. The voice then instructed me to take notice of the gnats hovering over the water of the stream. "Do you see those gnats?" the voice asked me.

"Yes," I replied.

"Those are my gnats. If you kill any one of them, you will disrupt the entire balance of nature. If they are that important to me, then how important do you think you must be?"

My mind instantly went back to the day while sitting at the kitchen table with my grandmother, when that strange-looking bug came to the window. I thought to myself, "Maybe it had come to pray for me, and I killed it."

Then, the voice continued, "You have no right to kill yourself. Someday, somebody is going to need you." Then, the voice was gone and I became keenly aware of my surroundings. The world instantly appeared to be a beautiful place. I now wanted to live in it and to remain a part of it for as long as possible. I looked up to the sky. Although I did not see anyone, I said, "Thank you," to the man on the cloud. It was there that I came to the realization that my life is determined by my own choices, and I choose to live my life to the best of my ability, every minute of every day. My life is worth living.

Chapter 7
MY SAFETY NET HAS A HOLE IN IT

Life makes some strange turns. You never know what event is about to happen in your life or which way that event is going to take you. Life is like riding a roller coaster.

I can remember working in a dental laboratory in Lake Hopatcong, New Jersey, for a man named Ricky Lumbrowski. The view of the lake presented itself from the front door of the laboratory. I often thought to myself about how nice it could be to live in that city for the rest of my life, if it just had not been for the obvious issue of poor race relations.

The entire scene, not just the scenery, but everything about Lake Hopatcong was like reading my life from a novel. Every novel has its antagonist. Sometimes, he is the hero; and sometimes, he is the villain.

Ricky was a decent enough man. Ricky, his wife, and their son Patrick worked there. I was the black sheep among them. But all in all, they tried to make me feel as comfortable as possible. But, Ricky was a very meticulous man. He wanted everything to be perfect. I didn't have a problem with that. I realize quality is important, especially in that line of work. What bothered me most about Ricky was the way he would talk down to me. One day I let him know just how I felt.

"You can't talk to me like that!" I shouted. "You need to edit your thoughts before you publish them. You need to think about what you are getting ready to say to me and how you are going to say it before you say it." My tone sounded strange to me, so I can only imagine Ricky's astonishment.

He tried to look tough before his two-person audience, as he shouted back, "I'm your boss," Ricky rebutted, "I talk to you the same way I talk to Pat."

"Yes," I snapped back. "But the difference between Pat and me is this: Pat is your son. I'm not your son. And you are not my boss. You are my customer. I am here to sell you a service. If you are not happy with my service, just say so, and I'll sell it to your competitor."

Then, I quoted a scripture, which I don't usually do. I said, "In my father's house are many mansions. If this were not so, I would not have told you." (John 14:2) I could tell by the way Ricky's entire demeanor changed that I had made him uncomfortable. But, I did not care. I was on a roll. So, I continued and said, "I was looking for a job when I found this one."

As the day went by, it was so quiet in Ricky's Dental Laboratory you could hear a fly urinate on cotton. When the day ended, Ricky came over to me and apologized. He said that he didn't mean to offend me. I told him that it was alright and that I didn't mean to lose my temper. Everything about Lake Hopatcong changed that day: the mood in the city and the picturesque scenery. I knew it was time for me to move on and that it would all soon become a distant memory. I was standing in the last paragraph before the beginning of a new chapter of my life's story, and I had already turned the page.

OK! I'll be the first to admit it. I lost my temper with Ricky, and it may have costed me a good job and possibly a good future. But, what is it worth without my self-respect? I personally refuse to get along with my oppressor. You cannot belittle me with smug remarks and expect me to put up with it, definitely not for a job. There is no room in the marketplace or in a free society for that type of behavior. So, I punched a hole in my own safety net, and I said to myself and to whomsoever might have been listening, "I am out of here!"

I just looked up toward the midnight, starlit sky as I had become accustomed to doing. I listened to my inner voice speak these words to me: "Follow the signs."

Chapter 8
FOLLOW THE SIGNS

I often think about how I entered into the field of dentistry. I was a teenage father at the tender age of fifteen years old. Up until my son was born, I had no thoughts of my future other than getting my driver's license and buying a big fancy car. But, the birth of my son created a paradigm shift in my way of thinking.

I looked around me and I thought my friends were either going to college or into the military. However, I was going to need a job because I had a child to feed and to provide for. My needs were immediate.

I realized the public school system was not going to equip me with what I needed to be a father, so I went to night school and took the only course I could take without a high school diploma. There was one other choice that I was left with. I could have studied barbering. Looking back, I don't know why I didn't. I guess, at the time, Dental Laboratory Technology sounded more professional. In any event, I chose that path. I worked with what was within my reach.

I was on the right track as far as securing employment,

but my personal life was still raggedy as a slice of Swiss cheese. I was living at home with my mother and my stepfather Frank. Frank was a nice guy. He did the best he could with what he had. But, he made me feel like I was in the way. Sometimes, I would hear him and my mother in their room arguing about my son and me. Frank would say things like, "When is he and his brat moving out?" That would really hurt me because I felt like I was paying my way. I knew that even though I was working, I wasn't making anywhere near enough money to move out on my own.

I sat out in front of my parents' house with tears in my eyes asking God, "Why is it God that you have allowed me to be in this situation? My sister and my brothers all have a home and a family, and here I am with nothing but a raggedy, old, beat up, lime green 1964 Ford Falcon."

As always, God spoke back to me. And what he said to me in that moment changed my life, and I often think back on His words. He said, "Show me that you appreciate what I have given you, and I will give you more than you can imagine."

The very next day, I took that funny-looking, beat up, raggedy, lime green 1964 Ford Falcon to a local body shop and had it painted black. It already had a black vinyl roof and black leather bucket seats. I transformed that car into something that caught the eye of passerby after passerby, who of course made me offers that I rejected without a thought.

I eventually started doing freelance work for various dental laboratories. One of my coworkers, who became a close friend of mine, opened a laboratory. We will call him Philippi Parker. I worked for Philippi part-time, along with about three or four other laboratories during that time. Philippi became one of my most dearest and lifelong buddies. He is the hardest working person I know and I give him credit for some of the best moves I have ever made in my life.

Chapter 9
I AM OUT OF HERE

I began dating again. It was strange at first because I noticed that I was no longer dating girls, but women. I had been so busy working I hadn't noticed the change in myself. I was now a young man and it was only appropriate that I would be keeping the company of young women. Although I enjoyed their company and the way they made me feel, I recognized that they were with me for more than just my company. They were with me because they saw a hardworking man in me.

After getting involved with a few undesirable, strange women, I became selective as to what I wanted in a woman. I quickly realized that it is senseless to work, if you are going to throw your money away trying to entertain people who presented themselves to you as friends. In actuality, they are only in your life to get what they can out of you. So, I quickly developed a budget and started setting both short, as well as long-term goals.

I borrowed money and rented a luxury apartment with a swimming pool on a hill in North Plainfield with a young lady and her daughter. It was with hopes that we could take our broken homes and make a family. Bridget turned out to be a pot-smoking bisexual who had no interest in anything other than her immediate pleasures. One day, she came home around three o'clock in the morning, just before daybreak. It wasn't the first time. We had argued about it on several occasions. I told her, "Bridget, I don't have a problem with you going out and hanging out in the streets as late as you want to, but you can't be coming into my house at all hours of the night." I warned her that if she didn't put a stop to it, "Some other woman is going to be switching in your kitchen."

Just like I made a budget for my finances to help me manage my personal expenses, I took inventory that morning on the qualities I wanted in the woman I wanted to share my life with. I knew that whomever I brought into my life was going to have a direct effect on my son's life. Never mind what she looks like. I needed a Christian woman in my life, someone who thought about the consequences of their actions. I needed a woman who had a job and a willingness to get up every morning and go to work. I didn't want a woman who smoked or drank more liquor than I did. She had to either be a homeowner or have a desire to own her own home. My grandmother used to say, "People who don't care, don't have a home." The inversion of that statement is simple. If they cared, they would either have a home or be doing all they can to get one.

Bridget took my warnings as idle threats. She thought she had me trapped in debt, and she did. But, like my mother, I often use anger as energy. Without giving it a second thought, I put her out. I packed her belongings and put them on the curb. "If you want to be in the streets so badly, you can live there. But, I am not trying to live there with you," I told her.

The apartment was in my name. We were three months behind in rent. I was working two jobs to get caught up. She was spending my money before I got it. Putting her out was the hardest thing I had done in my life up until that time. But, it was about survival. She would have to find her own way. I couldn't let her displace my son and me. She went back home with her mother; and I moved on with my life.

Chapter 10
MOVING ON

I finally did meet a woman who became my life partner, my wife. I recognized her the moment we met. Although she was working as a waitress in a cocktail lounge, she didn't have a cigarette dangling from her lips accompanied with foul language, nor did she drink liquor. I introduced myself to her, shook her hand, and attempted to suck her knuckle. She quickly snatched her hand away from me, as I would expect any decent young woman to do.

After talking with her for a few minutes, I told her that I am sure that a lot of guys approach her in a place like this. I told her I found her to be very interesting and I would like to see her again and possibly take her out for breakfast, lunch, dinner, or all of the above. Then, I gave her my telephone number and I told her that I was not going to take the chance of her giving me the wrong number. "If you are nearly as interested in us seeing each other again as I am, you will give me a call," is what I told her.

I was really surprised by my own exhibit of confidence, considering the fact that I had just gotten out of a destructive relationship. In our brief encounter, I discovered that she was a schoolteacher and studying Early Childhood Development. In addition to all of that, she had a daughter and she was a homeowner. I knew she was a woman of substance; the kind of woman who I would have been honored to marry. But, I wasn't sure if I would hear from her again or not, and I knew I wasn't going to go sniffing around her job trying to convince her that I was the man for her.

But, low and behold, she called me a few nights afterwards, around 11:01 p.m. I was asleep and I really didn't recognize her voice at first. When it became clear to me who she was, I asked her why she waited so late at night to call me. She said that she was waiting for the rates to go down.

I just smiled to myself and realized that she was thrifty; another good sign. We dated for a while and within one year we got married. After what happened between Bridget and me, I knew that I wasn't going to ever be comfortable living in someone else's house. So, one of the stipulations of my son and me moving out of our apartment and moving in with her was that she would have to sell her house and we would buy a larger one together, which we did.

My reason for bringing all of this up is to say that

although marriage is personal, it is a business deal. That is why you have to sign a contract when you get married. If you don't handle your personal life with care and it is a mess, there is no way your business life can be in order. I am not saying that my wife and I have a perfect marriage. We have certainly had our challenges, but I really believe she is the perfect wife for me.

My mother-in law, Evelyn Parker, God bless her soul, at around the same time that I quit my job at Ricky's Dental Laboratory, reconnected with a Baptist preacher named Reverend Eddie Capers. They hadn't been in touch with each other since their college days. Mrs. Parker had been a widow for over twenty years. She and Reverend Capers had a brief courtship, and then they married.

Once married, Mrs. Capers decided to move to Greenville, South Carolina, with her newly wedded husband; which was the right thing to do. But then, she began to talk with her two daughters, Dorothy, my wife, and Loretta, who is my sister-in law, about moving to South Carolina. At first, I thought that was not the right thing to do. However, instead of me taking the defense, I saw it as an opportunity to get away from people like Ricky, Leonard Bloomberg, and all of the other dental laboratory owners in New Jersey.

These laboratory owners seemed to monopolize the business, at least to the point where they controlled prices, wages, and even the lives of their employees. I have always been a nonconformist. That was my real motive for accepting Dorothy's proposal to move to South Carolina. My friends were telling me they would never marry a woman who has more education than they did or a better paying job. I figured if I was to marry a woman as broke as I was, we might both perish in poverty together. After all, doesn't the Holy Bible say that a woman is supposed to be her husband's helpmate, and not the other way around?

In the fall of 1988, we all headed south for a new life. I knew that I would miss my mother, my sister, and my brothers, but I needed out of New Jersey. And at that time, I figured this might be a good move.

Years after I moved from New Jersey, I learned that the construction of the New Jersey Turnpike began in 1952, the same year I was born. Somebody must have known way back then that I was going to want out.

Chapter 11
JUMP STREET

I grew up hard. Being the fourth child of five in a single parent household leaves a kid with little to no advantages. But, I learned early in life that money makes a difference and success is not determined by how much you have, but by what you do with what you have. I learned to play the hand that was dealt to me; and play the hand, I did.

We lived in a two and a half family house on the borderline street between poverty and prosperity. No kidding. The railroad tracks were right there; practically our next door neighbor. Whenever the train passed our house, the windows would vibrate, rattle, and shake right along with the rest of the house. We became so accustom to the train passing by every night at the same time, 11:15 p.m. When it didn't pass by, the silence would be so loud until it would wake everybody in the house. If you were to walk a quarter mile in either direction, you would be in the town of Glen Ridge. It was like living in hell, but directly across the street from Paradise. You could see luxury, but you could not touch it. It was so tantalizing.

Years later, in my adult life, I visited Alcatraz Federal Prison in San Francisco, California. It reminded me of those years growing up in Montclair, NJ, because of the way Alcatraz was situated; making San Francisco visible to the inmates on Alcatraz Island. San Francisco had been home to many of the inmates. Perhaps, being able to see home and not return must have been tantalizing to them. It may have been easier to live behind a wall than to have to experience such humiliation. That is what my childhood was like.

Glen Ridge sort of surrounded the street that we lived on where I grew up. It was an old community of wealthy Italians. They also owned most of Montclair. As a matter of fact, the house we lived in was owned by an Italian named Mike Fernando. I'll tell you more about him later.

On the first floor of the house where I began my formative years lived an old man named Hershel Navels. Somehow or another, Hershel became my best friend. If there were ever an odd couple, we were it. To someone standing by and looking at us in passing, they may have seen us as a grandfather and grandson on an outing. But, for people who knew us, they knew that there was something unusually strange about our friendship.

Mr. Hershel was a loud mouth gambler who sometimes drank too much. On the rare occasions when he would lose, he would become loud and obnoxious. The more he would lose, the more booze he would drink. And the more booze he drank, the more he would lose. In his sober moments, he would lecture me on the craft of gambling. He taught me how to recognize the signs of a mark and how to entice someone into a game of chance, in which the odds would always be in favor of the houseman.

I probably would have never met Hershel had it not been for the twist of fate my mother encountered. First, it was the separation from my father, then the death of my grandmother. My mother was left alone with nobody to help her with the support of her children. We went from living in a cold water flat on Oswald Place in Vaux Hall, New Jersey, at the mouth of what was once Bam's Woods to a tenement apartment on Morris Avenue in the slums of Newark. It was hard times for my mother. There had been rumors and tales of murderers hiding in Bam's Woods. But, there was nothing left to the imagination on the streets of Newark, New Jersey.

I have to give my mother credit though. She pulled us up from out of that degrading life, and she did it with style and finesse. My mother, Susan Elizabeth Bailey

Gibson, and now Preston, went to school, learned to become an LPN, and began private duties in the house of rich white people. Now, when I say rich, I'm talking Brookenridge, Fernando, and Graziani rich. My mother became so busy until she developed more customers than she could handle. She then trained my two aunts, Jean and Bernice, to fill in for her on various assignments. My mother was the first entrepreneur that I have ever known.

In the shadows of all success lurks a thief. This thief can come in many forms. When my mother landed a job looking after Mike Fernando's daughter, who had just given birth to his new grandson, he offered her an apartment living in a middle class, mixed neighborhood. The address was 91 Bay Street, Montclair, New Jersey. If I live to be a thousand years old, I will never forget that house. It was like the beginning of a new life for my mother and all of us. Life got better, but progress came with a price.

Chapter 12
THE MAN DOWNSTAIRS

Hershel Navels lived in the apartment on the first floor. He was an olive complexioned man who wore casual but expensive clothes. Hershel sported a nine-diamond cluster pinky ring and a gold tooth in the center of his mouth.

My two older brothers, Chuck and Bruce, along with a couple of friends that we had met named Joe Pelham and Butch Hopson, and I were sitting on the front porch playing twenty-one blackjack one hot Saturday morning when Hershel pulled up with his canary yellow Chrysler New Yorker.

Hershel reached into his pocket and pulled out a hand full of change. "How much is it gon' cost me for you fellas to keep an eye on my car and make for sure nobody mess with it." He handed each of us two quarters apiece. I spotted a couple of silver dollars in his hand and I told him, "I want the big money." He laughed and repeated what I had said, "I want the big money." Then, he put the money back in his pocket and walked into his apartment. I didn't know it at the time, but Hershel would eventually notice me more and

would take me under his wing. He actually asked my
mother if he could adopt me. Jokingly, she said yes.
But, when he showed up with the adoption papers for
her to sign, she said, "Man, you must be crazy."
I was just a kid shining shoes in Friendly's Barbershop
at 215 Bloomfield Avenue in Montclair, New Jersey,
trying to make a few dollars to help my single mother.
Little did I know, my life would be forever changed, for
better or worse, that summer evening in 1965 when I
asked Mr. Russell for a job shining shoes, sweeping the
floor, and cleaning drunk men's piss from the brim of
the toilet seat brought on by an effortless,
noncompetitive attempt of hit and miss.

When I first started working at the Barbershop, I was a
shy, quiet thirteen-year-old. In fact, I was so shy, I was
afraid to ask Mr. Russell for the job. I asked Horse
Johnson, my next-door neighbor, an older boy, to ask
Mr. Russell for me.

Mr. Russell asked me if I knew how to shine shoes. I
told him that I did. And it was true. I had experienced
shining shoes with my two older brothers, Chuck and
Bruce. We had worked the streets and bars of Vaux
Hall and Newark, New Jersey. Our grandfather on my
father's side of the family had given his shoeshine box
to Chuck. The three of us would go out together and
shine shoes. While one would shine a customer's shoes

the other two of us would stand guard to make sure none of the bigger kids and sometimes even the adults would come up and try to take our money.

I learned to clean from watching and sometimes assisting my mother clean the house. So, cleaning around the house and shining shoes on the streets were my basic training for Corporate America.

The shoeshine stand at Friendly Barbershop was made of marble, like a grave's headstone. I thought I had died and gone to shoeshine heaven. No more shining shoes on my knees.

Most of the men, with the exception of the drunkards, who usually came in around closing time on Friday night were generous. They gave me tips. Randolph and the other barbers would give me money for running errands and for keeping the floor around their chairs swept clean of hair. They gave me extra for cleaning their mirrors and countertops.

I had no way of knowing that I was being prepped for a life that would give definition to my youth, nor did I know that the errands I ran were for the illegal numbers game. I would pick up a slip of paper from beauticians, gas station attendants, dry cleaner workers, or anybody who wanted to participate in a game of chance. I was vaguely aware that my life had suddenly become eventful and I often dreamed of someday writing a book about that time in my life. I was too young and too naïve to even notice that when Randolph would send me to the restaurant to pick up a $2.50 ham and cheese sandwich, I would return with more change than the sandwich costed. I was delivering payoffs and didn't even know it.

Money started coming my way from every direction. I started buying gifts for my mother and my siblings. I bought my own clothes too, which freed my mother's purse of that expense. That is, in part, how I got the nickname *Midget*. Since I bought my own clothes, I bought what I wanted to wear, and what I wanted to wear were clothes that were too grown for a boy my age. I would buy Panama hats, pointed toed and wing tipped shoes, and bell-bottom pants.

One June afternoon when the sun was high in the sky, Hershel came into the barbershop in an attempt to shake Randolph down. He accused Randolph of owing him money for a number he claimed he had played and hit. Randolph was a barber, a number taker, and one of the most personable guys I have ever known; definitely a stranger to no one. But, he stood his ground with Hershel. He told Hershel that he had not played a number with him and he did not owe him a dime. Those number takers could recall numbers that they stored in their heads for weeks. Had they been given the opportunity that a lot of people have today, they could have been successful accountants and businessmen.

I was shining a customer's shoes when the confrontation began. Whenever James Brown or Smokey Robinson or some soulful artist of the day would come on the Juke Box when I shined shoes, all the barbers would stop cutting their customer's hair because they knew I would need a minute to pop my rag to the rhythm and the beat. They didn't want to make the mistake of jumping and nicking customers with the razor or cutting a patch of hair off their heads accidentally.

Although Hershel had given me the nickname, *Midget*, because of my grown man appearance and my little boy stature, Randolph called me *Beetle* because of the way I sometimes combed my hair. He said I reminded him of the Beetles. Randolph would mumble, "*Beetle*, *Beetle*, *Beetle*."

"Damn!" Hershel shouted, "Listen to that little man pop that rag." That was the second time I had encountered Hershel. He smiled, flashing his gold tooth while he rubbed his palm across his face, revealing his nine-diamond cluster on his pinky finger. Everything about Hershel radiated success in my mind, and I wanted to know exactly what it felt like to be that successful.

"When you grow up, you gonna be a hustler just like me. Because when I was your age, I was a hustler just like you," Hershel told me, pointing with his index finger, so there could be no mistake as to who he was talking to.

Then, Hershel walked out without saying anything to Randolph or anyone. A drunk mumbled, "When I die, who they gon' bury, me or you? If you don't want to die for me, then don't try to live for me."

Nobody paid any attention to the drunk. I assumed he was responding to Hershel's accusation.

The Roots of an Entrepreneur

I'M A HUSTLER

*I'm a hustler
Been a hustler since I was preteen
Hustle like a crackhead
But live like a king.*

*Never had a Daddy
But I have two brothers
We were like a Daddy
To each other.*

*We'd hit the cities' blocks
With our shoeshine box
Shine shoes on our knees
So the family could feast
On franks and beans.*

*The old man broke camp
Threw dirt on the fire
 Long before
 I even knew desire
To get out of the crib
Baby Brother was still in Mama's womb
I'm surprised any of us survived,
But we all did.*

That's why I hustle like a crackhead
But I live like a king.

Hershel's words stuck in my head. They were like a ray of sunlight that I would use to reflect on my life's path. Hershel had the flash, as well as the cash. I was intrigued, mesmerized, and damn near hypnotized by Hershel's charm. I took to Hershel like a fly takes to dung. Little did I know, but I soon discovered, I was about to fall into the counsel of a madman who would mark me for the rest of my life.

Chapter 13
THE HOUSEMAN ALWAYS WINS

Hershel started having card and dice games at his apartment. I used to hear his crowd laughing and cursing until the early hours in the morning. My mother would be out doing her twenty-four hour nursing duty and I would be home alone. I would go downstairs and just walk in Hershel's apartment. I walked around looking at all the money on the tables. Usually, no one would notice me. At least they didn't say anything directly to me. I would just sit in a corner quietly and watch. Hershel always won.

One morning around 9:00, after all the losers had left Hershel's apartment, it was just Hershel and me. "Ha, Big Money," Hershel recognized my presence. "How long you been sitting there?"

"All night," I answered. Then I asked him, "How'd you do that?"

"Do what?" Hershel asked with a big grin on his face that looked like he was going to burst out into laughter any minute.

"Come on Hershel. Nobody is that lucky. How did you keep winning like that?" Hershel began laughing a laugh that could have easily been confused with the devil's laughter, and then he said, real serious like, "Do you really want to know?"
I said, "Yes!" with conviction.

Hershel probably would have normally taken a shower, shaved, gotten a bite to eat, and gone to bed after such a long night. But instead, he sat up and lectured me on the art of gambling. He taught me how to roll seven with a pair of dice whenever I wanted to and how to crap out to let the losers win. "You have to let the losers win sometimes, just to keep them in the game. If they don't think they can win, they will quit, and then you can't beat them out of their money. You have to let them win sometimes."
Hershel sat up with me until about 3:00 that following afternoon. He laughed that devilish laugh again, and he said, "You know something Little Man, we gon' make a hell of a team. You gon' make more money than you ever dreamed of." And I did.

I didn't see Hershel for a couple of weeks after he gave me my introduction into gambling. Then, one morning about 4:00, I took a walk to Bloomfield Avenue where he would sometimes go to gamble. I was afraid to stay home alone. For some unknown reason, I felt safer on the avenue among those old gamblers and who knows what else, than I did in my own home.

Hershel owned a shoeshine parlor on the avenue called Majestic Shoe Shine Parlor. He was standing out in front of the building cursing to himself, as he sometimes would do. His eyes were bloodshot red. Looking into them were like peeping through the windows of hell and witnessing satan's fiery furnace for the first time. I instinctively became keenly aware that my best friend Hershel Navels was a dangerous man and that maybe I should keep my distance from him.

I asked him, "What's the matter, Hershel?" in my childlike tone, which I guarded from most people.

"Those no good lowlifes cheated me out of all of my money."

His true speech has been edited for the sensitivity of the readers' possible level of tolerance.

I asked him, "How do you know they cheated?"

Hershel looked at me for a sober minute, and then his expression suddenly changed as if he had just noticed that I was the dumbest person on earth. Hershel abruptly said, "Because I was cheating and they won. They must have been cheating."

I later found out that Hershel lost his shoeshine parlor that night in a dice game.
Hershel used to talk to himself in my presence and I would listen attentively to his rambling. I was eavesdropping on the private thoughts of a deranged man. One day Hershel was cursing under his breath saying, "People are going to call you a no good son of a so and so no matter what you do. It is better to be a rich one than a poor one."

I didn't know if Hershel's ramblings were meant for me to hear or not. Whether they may have been or not, I listened attentively and I took it all in. In my mind, then and now, Hershel was one of the few geniuses I have ever had the pleasure of knowing, though he was a little crazy at the same time, as is most geniuses.

One day I witnessed Hershel bet and lose five hundred dollars on what I thought to be a dumb bet. There were two sparrows sitting on a telephone wire. Hershel bet a man named Eighty-One, a fellow gambler, that the bird on the left would take flight before the bird on the right. When the bird on the right took flight first, Hershel reached into his pocket, pulled out a bankroll, peeled off five one hundred dollar bills like leaves from an onion, and handed them to Eighty-One.

"That was a dumb bet," I shouted in protest. "I thought you said not to gamble but to take calculated risks." I reminded Hershel of his own words of wisdom.

Hershel tried to be patient with me because he knew I was developing skills that he was teaching me. He was capitalizing on me as well, and he did not want to offend me. Hershel had actually taught me skills of the street life.

"That was a calculated risk," Hershel shouted. "Look! I had a fifty-fifty chance to win. How many times have you ever known a black man to get a fifty-fifty chance with anything?"

Hershel used to tell me to always have someplace to go to get some more chips whenever your chips were low and you need to get back in the game. That was the kind of advice Hershel gave me. The year was 1965. The turbulent sixties were an exciting time for a black youth in any city in America. I am now almost as old as Hershel was back then and I have to admit, the sixties were the most exciting times of my life. It was for me as adventurous as the times of Huckleberry

Finn must have been for Mark Twain.

During those days, with the Civil Rights Movement, the assassination of JFK, Martin Luther King Jr., Malcolm X, and all the other unrest, I wondered about what my mother had said about my great-grandfather and what became of him. Back in those days, there was no black history being taught in the segregated black schools, with the exception of those few black teachers who were brave enough to take pride in their race. My third and fourth grade teachers, Ms. Hudson and Ms. Steward, were such brave souls.

I had questions that I needed answered. So, I collected myself and went to visit my father. My father and I, up until that time were not close, in any sense of the word. I remember the night he and my mother broke up. He left my older sister Antoinette, my two older brothers, along with my pregnant mother and me. I could not have been older than four or five years old. I never understood the motive behind his decision.

He was surprised to see me the few times I would come around. This visit was different because I came with questions about my great-grandfather. He immediately went into denial mode when I told him what my mother had said about my father's grandfather being a human breeder. He and my mother still had not reconciled. He did not have anything to say nice about her, and he never said anything bad about her either. Their sentiments towards each other were mutual.

I started recognizing a similarity in Hershel, my father, and all black men. Although I couldn't quite figure out the relationship, there was definitely something identical about them. My father must have detected my desperate determination to know my grandfather's father's story, because he sat me down and we had our first man-to-man talk.

Some people are strong enough to be victorious in battle. Some are wise enough to know when to retreat. While others are foolish enough to perish in defeat.

Chapter 14
MIDNIGHT THUNDER

The Cherokee Indians called him Midnight Thunder because he would ride his horse from the south of the border all the way through Cherokee, North Carolina. He would yell and curse the night all the way into the early morning, rounding up and herding wild horses while their hooves beat against the earth all the way to the Gibson Plantation.

He was the only slave in those parts who had such liberties. Some wondered why he never attempted to escape, but John Wesley saw the Gibson Plantation as his camp, a place to go when he became weary of roaming. Matt gave John a thirty-day pass each month, with the understanding that if he was to ever violate his privileges, he would be haunted down and killed. John knew not to test his master's prophecies. Besides, he had sweat equity in the plantation, and his master, Matt Gibson, who all the slaves on the Gibson Plantation were named after, had equity in him. John Wesley was feared yet respected and he felt a certain responsibility towards his master, as well as the tenants of the plantation despite the fact that the overseer of the plantation, Jim Frierson and John Wesley shared a mutual hatred towards each other.

John was a herder. There was not a horse that he could not break, no matter how wild the horse might have been. John would mount the most ferocious of horses, and within a matter of minutes, he would have it eating oats out of his hand. John was also a blacksmith and a hunter.

The only thing he did not do was pick cotton. That is where he and Jim had conflict, because Jim demanded obedience from the slaves that were put in his custody. John refused to pick any cotton. The only thing that John's master demanded of him was that he mated with the young virgins, as well as the wenches and put a baby in their bellies. He said it was their rites of passage into womanhood. But if the truth is to be told, every offspring that passed through John Wesley's groin was worth $5000 to Matt Gibson. John stood almost seven feet tall. He was a solid two hundred and fifty pounds of rare stock.

Matt's only demand was John's greatest resentment. John did not have any problem with breeding with the older wenches, as they were called. Some of them actually found pleasure in being with John, and John with them. But, because John had fathered so many children, too many for him to keep an account of, he dreaded that type of demand his master charged him with. It was always dreadful for him, and occasionally, fatal for the girl.

The ritual was always the same. A team of new slaves would be brought onto the plantation that old master Gibson had either bought or bartered for. The men, women, and children slaves were immediately introduced to the cotton field. The newly born would be harnessed to their mother's back while she picked. There was no minimum or maximum age for the field, unless it could be proven by the slave to his master that they were of greater value in some other venue. Those women who were of childbearing age would be ushered into the barn where John lived with his horses, almost as quickly as the others were taken to the field.

One evening, just before dusk, John was grooming the horses while he cooked a wild rabbit over an open fire. It was drizzling a cold, light rain when Jim Frierson, the plantation's overseer, entered the barn, dragging with him a frightened girl, not big as a colt, behind him. Jim shoved the child to John's feet with a distorted grin on his face. "Breed her!" he ordered, with the casualness of one ordering a brand on an animal, as he turned and walked out, leaving the two slaves to do their do.

John could feel the temperature rise throughout his

body. It was not lust for the girl. He had no desire for children; it was hatred for Jim. He had promised himself that someday he would kill Jim, but he knew that if and when that day was to ever come, he would have to abandon any thoughts of ever returning to the Gibson Plantation. He began formulating a plan in his head.

The girl sat by the fire, terrified. She knew from the older women what was to come. They told her, "It will be the worse pain you have ever experienced in your life. It is going to feel like you are on fire from your stomach to your toes. The only thing more painful is having a baby, which you will also experience if he gets you pregnant. And if he doesn't, he will do it to you over and over again and again until he knocks you up. Eventually, you will learn to like it."

The girl just sat, watching John's every move, and thinking about what all the older women had told her. Despite the fact that the girl was barely covered with nothing but a rag for a dress, exposing her youthful buds, John's mind was on something else. To the girl, he seemed to be in deep thought.

It was damp and cold in the barn and smelled of horse manure; something that never occurred to him before. But, with the girl, he thought to himself, "She should not be here." He suddenly became aware of the girl, regaining his full consciousness of his surroundings. When the girl made eye contact with John, while she sat on the ground, she scooted backwards and away from him. John remained silent. When he finally spoke, he asked the girl, "You hungry?"

She nodded her head up and down to indicate that she was, in fact, hungry. He knelt down by the open fire, cut off a chunk of flesh from the rabbit, and handed it to her on the knife's tip. As the girl took the knife with the flesh hanging off its tip, she instinctively considered using the knife to defend herself. John must have known what she was thinking. He also must have known that she must have known that the consequence of her resisting him would be punishable by their master. He also must have known that if he showed compassion for the girl and disobeyed his master's demand, he, as well as she would have been beaten with the whip to the bare bone.

The tenants of the plantation listened attentively, waiting to hear the screams. But the anticipated screams never came. John decided the time had come. He told the girl, "Don't be afraid. I am not going to hurt you. Eat. Get some rest. We have a long ride ahead of us in the morning." The girl didn't utter a word. She just ate and then curled up by the fire and slept through the night. John sat with his back against the wall watching the girl sleep until he too dosed off to sleep.

Just before daybreak, John unlocked all of the horses' stalls one by one. He mounted his horse with the girl and stirred the other horses into a stampede trampling Jim as they left the Gibson Plantation heading north for Indian Territory, against a cold, rain-filled morning.

Chapter 15
MOMMA DON'T TAKE NO MESS

I have always thought there was something exceptionally unique about a runaway slave. That may sound silly, but to attempt to escape the only way of life you know and to venture out into a world that you know absolutely nothing about because the only thing you know for certain about your life is that you don't like anything about it. That is a bold step on faith and it is to be commended.

It is synonymous to the life of an entrepreneur. You roll the dice. You take a chance. And you deal with the consequences of your own actions. Midnight Thunder knew his self-worth extended beyond picking cotton and being used for breeding. It was his true nature to roam and to hunt, but not to be anyone's possession. Some people fit right into submission, being controlled and told what to do. But, the rules are different for those with a warrior's spirit.

If you look back far enough, you can see tomorrow because life is a circle. I learned that truth from the many stories my father told me while sitting in his attic apartment on my many visits. The more he revealed to me, the more inquisitive I became. I wanted to know what became of Midnight Thunder and the girl. The more he talked, the better I came to understood myself.

My father told me that they settled on a Cherokee reservation for a few years. That is what a lot of the runaway slaves did. The Cherokee Indians were notorious for taking in runaway slaves. I guess they had a common enemy in the white man. John Wesley had escaped many times from various plantations, seeking refuge among the Indians until Matt Gibson bought him. Matt had treated John Wesley well and he probably would have spent the remaining years of his life on the Gibson plantation, had it not been for that ill-fated night when Jim, his heartless overseer, issued his order to "breed the girl."

John had allowed himself to be captured on many occasions and to be taken back onto the various plantations he had escaped, in spite of the harsh punishment he knew awaited him. He hated wandering alone. Although the Indians treated him like one of their own, he never felt the same kindred towards them that he felt with the tenants on the plantation.

My father paused at that point in his story and said, "I

can relate to that, Son. I have felt like an aimless drifter ever since your mother and I separated."

I could feel a sort of sorrow for my father when he said that. "Why did you and Mom break up?" I asked him with the same childlike tone that I used when I asked Hershel, "How do you know they cheated you?" I saw a similar expression on my father's face that I had seen on Hershel's face. I knew I had asked another one of those hard questions that grownups sometimes try to sidestep.

"Your mother," my father said, "was a lot like the girl that Midnight Thunder took a liking to. That girl became my father's grandmother. She was soft spoken and sweet like a lady, until she got angry. The Indians named the girl, Quiet Storm. That was your mother's way. She didn't like for me to discipline you kids. Whenever I tried, she became real protective of you all. I guess that is one of the traits of a mother that is passed down from generation to generation. There can only be one head of a household and your mother battled me for that position. One thing about the Indians, the chief always led their warriors into battle, but they never engaged in battle themselves. I learned to lead from a distance with hope that someday you would do as you have done. You have come to me as a warrior does to a chief, for counseling."

I recognized the resemblance that I saw in black men in my father during that conversation. It is the oppression and the isolation that black men feel that make them appear hard and compassionless. My father seemed to soften when he talked about my mother. I know that my momma can be a force to reckon with.

I later discovered that my mother also had a multicultural history. My grandfather on my mother's side of the family was Mexican. My grandmother ran him off. I guess the women in my family have always had a lot of fire in their blood.

What you don't have, you have to get.
Whatever you do, just don't quit.
Because all of your dreams are within your reach
Mothers and fathers
This is something to your children
You must teach.
But if you want to have them,
You have to grab them.

Yeah, I'm living like a pimp on crack
Chasing and catching destiny every day
And never looking back.
May God have mercy on the fool
who gets in my way.

JOHN LESLIE GIBSON

I'm a hustler
Been a hustler since I was preteen
Hustling like a crackhead
But live like a king.

Chapter 16
POISON IN THE WELL

I don't know how I feel about integration. Sometimes, I think it is a good thing to mix and match, and at other times, I feel like it is best to keep things separated, compartmentalized.

Like they say, "One bad apple can spoil the whole bunch." Rarely do you see different species of birds, cats, or dogs in the same pack. Maybe people, by nature, are designed to be tribal. Sometimes, it seems like we are all a part of a great big experiment. Maybe the Hindus are on to something. Pre-arranged marriage might work best.

"Father Knows Best" used to be a TV show that made some very good points. The father was the final decision maker in the family who all the kids and even the mother came to for advice. But, with fathers being absent, life is a guessing game, with the government making all the decisions for the family. If government really had the individuals' best interests in mind, this country as a whole wouldn't be so messed up.

Mr. Illuminati

All of that is behind me now. I am as old as Hershel and my father were way back then. With all I have learned from those days gone by, my life has become crystal clear to me. When my mood change, I realize that with the changing of my mood comes a change in my perspective. When I am at peace, the world appears to be a great big garden. But, when I become a bit agitated, the world becomes a jungle.

I realize a garden needs to be weeded occasionally. According to the scriptures of the Holy Bible, God created man to cultivate the Garden of Eden. When the weeds become out of control, the garden becomes similar to a jungle. It is hard to stay at peace with one's self in a forever-changing world where the weeds just keep on growing and distorting the minds and focus of God's people.

But, we must keep in mind that just as we may have a heritage that we are unfamiliar with, so too is it possible that we belong to a group of people that we are totally unaware of. The world is filled with secret societies. Occults keep appearing across the land and we can easily become indoctrinated without even knowing. Our belief system makes us a part of something too huge to recognize, like the forest to the trees.

That is why it is important to be fearless and to accept one's own individuality and not be afraid to stand out. We should not try to be like everybody else or try to get in where we fit in with the crowd. We must find our own light from within ourselves and stand out. The majority of the inhabitants of this world will die penniless and go straight to hell. Why would anyone desire to be part of such a crowd? Just because you are in the world, does not mean you are of it. Just because you know my name, doesn't mean you know me. After all, the name I go by might not even be my name.

ABOUT THE AUTHOR

John Leslie Gibson resides in Sumter, SC, with his

wife Doncella Gibson. He is semi-retired from the State of South Carolina where he has served in several positions of social service, as well as the health care industry. John is active in his community. He is also the proud father of three children, six grandchildren, and one great-grandchild.

The Roots of an Entrepreneur is John's first book, which was inspired by his daughter, Monique Sandiford, who is the author of her first children's book, Gimme Kimmy and the Wiz.

www.ingramcontent.com/pod-product-compliance
Lightning Source LLC
Chambersburg PA
CBHW021959290426
44108CB00012B/1131